BAAS Pamphlets in Americ

Radical Theatre
in the Sixties and Seventies

Richard Walsh

British Association for American Studies

First Published 1993

© British Association for American Studies, 1993

ISBN 0 946488 14 2

Cover design by Ryburn Design
Composed and originated by Ryburn Publishing Services
Printed by Ryburn Book Production, Halifax, England

Contents

Introduction

The nature of radicalism in the theatre is complex: the aesthetic and political senses of radicalism are not easily reconciled, yet theatre is the art form in which aesthetics and politics are most inextricably linked. R.G. Davis, founder of the San Francisco Mime Troupe, addressed this issue in his 1975 article, "The Radical Right in the American Theatre": he distinguished the theatre of the radical left, which "engages in picket lines and demonstrations as part of its work", from that of the radical right, which "is an extension or a deviation from the bourgeois theatre, and is closely aligned with the aesthetic avant-garde".[1] Davis, as a partisan of the radical left he identifies with the San Francisco Mime Troupe, El Teatro Campesino and the Bread and Puppet Theatre, uses the distinction to repudiate the alternative radicalism of the Living Theatre, the Open Theatre and the Performance Group. All of these groups, and others, are considered in this pamphlet under headings that to some extent acknowledge the opposition proposed by Davis. But underlying these two apparently irreconcilable versions of radical theatre there is, I would suggest, a common set of assumptions and intellectual strategies that inform both political and aesthetic frames of reference. A sense of this fundamental orientation provides the means to understand both the strengths and weaknesses of radical theatre, and the nature of the tension between the two aspects of its radicalism.

I propose to deal with radical theatre groups in three categories. In the first are those who found the experimental theatre group as such to be a compelling model of the structural possibilities for society in a time of revolutionary political visions and proliferating countercultural lifestyles. As a central metaphor for the community as a whole, these theatre groups considered their own structure and working practices, as well as the form and content of their work, to have an exemplary function: their aesthetic principles reached towards political significance in every aspect of their organization. Theatre and its creative and performative activities became in itself a mode of living, expanding under the rubric of performance theatre into a radical subversion of many prevailing assumptions about the concept of theatre and the ways it is produced and experienced. Groups in the second category emerged from specific political contexts to serve political ends: in such cases the role of theatre itself was more narrowly defined, and its forms emerged in a dialectic with the causes they served. In these groups aesthetics followed from politics, rather than vice versa: but their political stance also evolved through this reciprocity between ideological and strictly theatrical considerations. Toward the end of the sixties the always latent individualism in the theatre's models of communality regained currency, allowing the emergence of a third radical orientation in which aesthetics obscured politics: the social and political dimensions of theatre were truncated to allow an exploration of the encounter between the theatrical medium and the individual perceiving mind.

In all these contexts radical groups confronted the web of formative dualisms that conventionally preside over the creation, production and reception of theatre: text and performance, stage and auditorium, performer and spectator, performer and character, action and dialogue, author and director, author and actor, art and life ... Generally, one term in these oppositions is privileged in establishment theatre, so that the other has a subordinate function, serving the ends of or operating within terms defined by its dominant partner. The characteristic feature of the aesthetics of the radical theatre was the attempt to resist the hegemony of many of these dualisms, and to substitute for them a *holistic* framework by which the inequity of the two terms is overcome. By holism I mean a disposition to reject dualistic models of related phenomena or concepts in favour of a gestalt interpretation which insists upon the unity of the whole and the presence in it of characteristics or values that are destroyed by dualistic (or atomistic) representations. The conceptual whole is regarded as irreducible either because the prevailing dualism is invalid or because it is unable to account for certain features of the whole. Accordingly, the intellectual process by which holistic ends may be approached takes one of two courses. It may *subvert* a prevailing dualism, denying its polarities and identifying qualities that manifest the continuity between them. Or, it may *transcend* the extant dualism, asserting a synthetic whole in which the opposed terms remain discrete but are united by qualities to which they have a common relation. In aesthetic terms, these two ways of overcoming hierarchical dualisms were often confused, yet they have very different outcomes. While transcendence achieves an ideal holism, subversion resolves itself into a reductive monism: by obliterating distinctions, a monistic framework can only consolidate or invert (depending which term absorbs the other) the inequality of its dualistic equivalent. The contemporary situation of radical politics involved an equivalent confrontation with those dualisms enshrined in the inequalities of the political establishment: but also, and much more immediately, it involved a repudiation of the *monistic* response implied by assimilationist and liberal reform. The overriding characteristic of sixties radical politics was therefore separatism, in apparent contradiction to the radical aesthetics with which it nonetheless shared an underlying holistic orientation.

The holistic predilections of the avant-garde theatre groups of the period have numerous analogues in the contemporary political, social, cultural and spiritual climate. In fact the diversity of forms in which such orientations are manifested makes the task of identifying sources extremely problematic. The complex interrelationship between the spheres of culture, politics and aesthetics blurs easy distinctions between the seminal and the symptomatic, and the means of adjudication are beyond the scope of this pamphlet; but certainly the evidence is abundant. Perhaps the most salient feature of the political climate of the fifties is the rigidification of ideological polarities consequent upon the Cold War: the Manichean extremes to which this led political rhetoric, together with its co-option as a tool of right wing conformism, demanded a radical response that questioned the framework itself. The necessarily holistic form such an anti-Manicheanism would take also needed to resist the ultimately monistic homogeneity of a rapidly advancing consumer culture. This was the essential point the New Left extracted from Herbert Marcuse's *One Dimensional Man*: that contemporary American mainstream culture had developed the capacity to absorb and negate all opposition, obliterating its contradictions in a monism driven by consumer materialism. The fragmentary structure of New Left radical resistance can be understood as resulting from this suspicion of coercive homogeneity, in relation to both the mainstream culture and the liberal co-option of Old Left causes.

The appeal of Zen to the counterculture of the sixties can also be considered in this light. It offered a means of redressing the alienation produced by the prevailing dualisms of self and community (exacerbated by competitive individualism) and mind and body (exacerbated by impotent intellectualism). Zen offered a radical reaffirmation of the unity of the practitioner with reality, a perspective accessible to the American sensibility perhaps in terms of a modern, secular transcendentalism. But it did not provide the means to distinguish between the monism of a pure obliteration of differences and the interrelation of discrete particles that would constitute a true holism, and to that extent, as with the emerging drug culture, risked losses as serious as its gains. Its influence is nonetheless undeniable, in the realm of art as much as in general culture. The overarching aesthetic imperative of the era, to overthrow the dualism of life and art, is a manifestly Zen aspiration.

If a single figure could be identified in which the aesthetics of holism were encapsulated, it would be John Cage. He was profoundly influenced by Zen – and indeed by Thoreau – and his presence in the history of avant-garde aesthetics is remarkable. Cage's redefinition of music as (potentially) all sound, and theatre as similarly latent in all visible and audible activity was a vitally enabling (and radically holistic) gesture. While at Black Mountain College, Cage introduced Artaud's *The Theatre and Its Double*, which was translated there by Mary Caroline Richards: when a copy came to the attention of Julian Beck and Judith

Malina at the Living Theatre, it precipitated the advent of performance theatre. In the summer of 1952, also at Black Mountain, Cage orchestrated an event retrospectively identifiable as an ur-Happening – a "concerted action" involving simultaneous piano, gramophone, poetry, dance, lecturing, films and slides. Later he taught courses in avant-garde music at the New School for Social Research in New York, and several of his students there made a subsequent impact upon avant-garde aesthetics: among them was Allan Kaprow.

The term "Happening" was taken from Kaprow's 1959 piece, *18 Happenings in 6 Parts*, performed for an invited audience in a Greenwich Village loft. The mixed-media performance events that became generically known as Happenings were one of the most vital influences upon the radical theatre of the sixties, but they originated in a series of logical extensions of the scope of art, and evolved towards theatre via a series of synthetic manoeuvres in a contemporary dialectic about the nature of the artwork. In terms of Kaprow's own artistic development, the emergence of the Happening can be charted through Assemblages and Environments, each category constituting an advance in the attack on prevailing dichotomies. Assemblages, by incorporating everyday objects into sculpture, breached the barrier between the artist's or spectator's own context and the realm of art. Environments, which redefined the artwork as the entire physical arena in which it was experienced, overcame the institutionalized anathema of the gallery space. The general thrust was towards a transcending of all categorical dualisms by which art was opposed to life. In the Happening, this objective was further served by a synthesis of the realms of vision and sound, of the static and the animated, and finally the observer and the participant.

Kaprow indicates that the process of composition remained the same throughout these mutations, being based upon collage, the juxtaposition of discrete elements designed to establish formal continuity with ordinary experience. Michael Kirby, in his introduction to the first (1965) anthology of Happenings, formalizes this characteristic as "compartmented structure", making it crucial to his definition of Happenings.[2] Compartmented structure implies composition with sequential or simultaneous discrete units, devoid of any narrative or causal connection. In Happenings it is linked with what Kirby calls "nonmatrixed performance" – the performance matrix being the imaginary dimensions of time, place and character created within the actual circumstances of conventional theatre. By remaining rigorously in the here and now the action of Happenings refused that duality, as another aspect of the divorce of life and art. Kirby highlights these characteristics to correct the common perception of Happenings as unscripted and improvised: the structural composition of a Happening was always clearly defined, whilst allowing great scope for chance occurrences within that framework; and the concept of improvisation implies ad hoc invention *within a matrix*, whereas Happenings are characterized by nonmatrixed indeterminacy. There are clearly elements of Dada and Surrealism in this preference for the illogical, collage and the operations of chance; but Kirby insists that the indeterminacy of Happenings should not be understood as a programmatic Dadaist attack upon reason, arguing that it is *alogical* rather than illogical (again, a holistic manoeuvre).

The convergence of art and theatre initially led to Happenings that adopted standard performance conventions, but this tended to truncate the implications of the form, the logic of which soon pushed it beyond theatre. So, Kaprow's summary of the essential characteristics of Happenings includes the fragmentation of the space and time in which they occur (so refusing the segregated space and time of art represented by an evening at the theatre). In the same way, the original concern with space and sound that prompted Kaprow's move into Happenings shifted towards a focus upon audience participation and response. The division between observers and participants had been undermined in the earliest Happenings: the audience were given the opportunity to participate, such audience involvement being provided for by the open structure of the Happening script. Ultimately, however, Kaprow proposed that "audiences should be eliminated entirely".[3] All those present at a Happening would be participants, and briefed as to the parameters of their role. Essential to this concept of the Happening is the non-professionalism of the performers: they do not in any sense lose themselves in a role, and so remain present to the immediacy of their perceptions and experiences. Such a criterion is indicative of the end to which the Happenings were gravitating: their synthesis of all elements of art and life, including the roles of participant and observer, eventually focussed all discrimination upon the one remaining duality – that between perception and the consciousness of it. The significance of the Happenings lies in this attention to perception. Their guiding principles always excluded the possibility of any sort of commentary upon life, and to the extent that they could be seen as imitations of their milieu (in their preference for everyday and junk materials, or principles of juxtaposition, for example) this was not a descriptive enterprise but an assertion of continuity. The objective was always to test and explore the nature of perception, not merely in an "artistic" context but as such, and above all to develop a sensitivity to its operations. But while the guiding concept of perception was holistic, the effort to remove their own status as art from the equation led to a monistic reductivism that denied the Happenings any analytical potential, and they quickly outlived the interest generated by their radical originality, becoming repetitive and ordinary. But given the rationale of a pedagogical mission – the siting of aesthetic experience as a faculty of perception in itself – the Happenings can be understood to have invented their own redundancy.

The Happenings exerted an enormous influence upon the direction of radical theatre in America in the sixties. Their aesthetic project, the location of aesthetic experience, of perception and the consciousness of it, at the heart of their performance rationale, signalled a major development in the idea of theatre as an aesthetic experience that was later to emerge in the "Theatre of Images". But more directly, their break with the established framework of performance conventions – the separation of performance and audience space, the passive audience – and their exploration of principles of immediacy in performance, multiple focus, variable time and action, and the displacement of language, all became essential concerns of those involved in performance theatre – through whom they gained even wider currency.

Performance Theatre

Radical theatre practice in the sixties developed in terms of at least four structural dualisms: actor and character; creation and performance; stage and auditorium; and theatre and life. A holistic approach to these oppositions produced "performance theatre", a concept that came to be defined by the work of three groups: the Living Theatre, led by Judith Malina and Julian Beck; the Open Theatre, led by Joseph Chaikin; and the Performance Group, under Richard Schechner.

The concept of the actor developed by these groups is exemplified in Schechner's objections to Method acting, and in particular the principle of "affective memory" or "emotional recall" in which an actor finds the emotion required for a particular scene by reliving an equivalent personal experience. The inadequacy of such an approach, he argues, is that it fails to retain both conviction and pretence in acting: "It is wrong to call a feeling aroused by affective memory an 'illusion'; physiologically it is exactly what it was the first time, only now it is an effect without its original cause".[4] This absence of illusion means in effect the obliteration of the actor in the character: it is acting as pure conviction. Affective memory therefore dichotomizes the elements of acting: conviction is absolute from the actor's interior perspective, the awareness of pretence having been displaced onto the preparatory technique. Schechner insists that conviction and pretence must be co-present within the actor's performance for the concept of acting to have its full meaning. Such co-presence retains the mimetic doubleness lost in Method acting, and is therefore the richer for the "surplus energy" of its simultaneity. He cites Brecht, and the "method of physical action" of late Stanislavski, neglected in American Method training: here the first principle is mimesis, containing both conviction and the awareness of role which is pretence: the actor is both involved and removed from the part.

In this model, the opposed terms "conviction" and "pretence" are held in suspension by a holistic concept of mimesis as self-conscious role play. But the holistic approach that motivated most of the innovations of these theatre groups was often confused with a monistic *collapse* of opposed terms: and this confusion transformed many of their gains into serious losses. If, instead of proposing a conceptual gestalt that contains the dichotomy between conviction and pretence, Schechner had proposed (as he might have done) a direct continuity between actor and character, neither one being the exclusive domain of "self" or "role", then again the actor's self-consciousness is the released third term, but this time it is immanent in both the others, and expresses their continuity. Such a model would not be the immersion of self *in* role of affective memory, nor the dialectic of self *and* role of the Brechtian model Schechner actually proposes. It would be the obliteration of any distinction between self and role, so that the two become simply coextensive and there is a loss of mediation between them.

The uneasy proximity of this second holistic stance to the first is apparent in Joseph Chaikin's writings on *The Presence of the Actor*, which take the form of notes written during his work with the Open Theatre.[5] Chaikin's thoughts on the actor were first stimulated while doing Brecht with the Living Theatre, but when he sought to extend his ideas in the context of the intensely and explicitly actor centred environment of the Open Theatre, a mutation in his attitude to Brecht occurred: Chaikin's actor's perspective substituted a continuity between the actor and the world for the actor's synthetic position as mediator between the play and the world, and so obliterated, rather than transcending, the dualism of art and reality. Self and role then form a continuum, not a dialectic: rather than the actor as the site of a mediation between self and role, we have the actor as a model of unified personality. The crucial influence is Grotowski's "Poor Theatre", which centred upon the internal resources of the actor: Grotowski found the Open Theatre, whose actors shared an exceptionally compelling presence with those of his own Polish Lab, the only American company worthy of his endorsement. But his explanation for the power of this presence also makes clear the cost: "It is because his nature has been unveiled. He is not divided between certain mental conceptions, that is to say, an intellectual 'me' and all the rest; he is a whole being. He is at the same time the spirit and the body, the sex and the intellect, the biology and the lucidity, and this 'and' is not this and that, it is all one".[6] The singularity of this "nature" leaves no room in such an actor for any dynamic interaction of conflicting elements: instead of mediation and synthesis, we have an absolute monistic whole. Such singularity is a source of power in performance, but also involves sacrifices that were apparent in the Open Theatre's *The Serpent* (1968).

The Serpent originated in acting exercises, but was organized around the story of Genesis, in particular the Fall and Cain and Abel. The first sequence of the play, however, is a reenactment of the assassination of President Kennedy. Two couples kneel onstage as in an open car. An "assassin-director", pointing an imaginary rifle toward the car, calls the numbers of twelve frames by which the action of the assassination is frozen into a series of iconic moments. The scene shifts instantly to the Garden of Eden. Five actors, holding apples in their hands, form both the Tree of Knowledge and the Serpent. When Eve and Adam have fallen into temptation, apples are scattered across the floor for the actors to gorge themselves upon; the fruit is also offered to the audience. The carnival atmosphere gives way to a crescendo of God's curses. Then comes the killing of Abel, methodically and ignorantly:

"And it occurred to Cain to kill his brother. But it did not occur to Cain that killing his brother would cause his brother's death".[7] The play ends with the "Begat" scene, in which the actors, to the intoning of the relevant verses of the Bible, discover each other and sex, and plunge into an enactment of mass copulation. Finally the men transform into children, the women into mothers, then all decline into old age and death. In dealing with this mythic material, the actors sought to break through the cliché images to find authentic personal references. The problem arises when this private authenticity has to be generalized: Chaikin insisted that collaborative work could elicit "deep common references", but such generalization depends upon a haphazard trial and error procedure arising from the group's commitment to an acting method based upon the integrity of the actor's personality. The resultant performance is therefore a fragile and highly contingent whole. Chaikin wrote in the program notes to *The Serpent*, 'Don't lose any thought wondering what connects the scenes or what logic applies from one scene to the other. The connections are in your head".[8] The considerable success of the production was attributable to its use of myth as an aid to this reconnection: it allowed the group to achieve a suggestive power that was universally acknowledged. But its non-explicitness was also a fundamental weakness: it rendered the work unable to elicit associations beyond the obvious and familiar. The personal projection of the actors' selves, while certainly the source of a general resonance, ultimately denied the play any objective framework and limited its capacity to analyze its own material.

The creative procedures used by the Open Theatre in constructing *The Serpent* are exemplary of the pressure towards a synthesis of artistic forces – a holistic approach to the creative process – that prevailed among those involved in performance theatre. There *was* a written text for *The Serpent*, and it was written by a playwright – Jean-Claude van Itallie – but the process by which this text was arrived at differed significantly from the conventional relationship between writer and performers, and from the Open Theatre's previous work with van Itallie. In writing *The Serpent*, van Itallie was present from the beginning of the group's improvisatory exercises, functioning less as the originator of the text than as its scribe, its recorder and orchestrator. Instead of a dualistic model in which the written text stands in opposition to the various aspects of its realization, the Open Theatre adopted a holistic creative method in which the function of playwright is coordinated with those of director, actor and designer into a single artistic endeavour.

This impulse was shared by many of the theatre groups of the time, manifesting itself in various degrees, from revisionary productions of standard texts to a total exclusion of the text as such. The former approach, practised by both the Living Theatre and the Performance Group in their appropriations of Sophocles and Euripides respectively (and generally confined to the work of safely dead playwrights) accorded with Grotowski's attitude to the dramatic text as pretext. The latter, textless strategy, most comprehensively adopted by the Living Theatre, took to heart Artaud's call to "renounce the theatrical superstition of the text and the dictatorship of the writer". [9] There was a certain disingenuousness about this call to creative unity, however: in many cases, underlying the superficial transfer of power to the coordinated collective artistic faculties of the theatre group, was a much more monolithic appropriation of the authority of the writer by the director. Despite the Living Theatre's organization as an anarchistic collective, its domination by Beck and Malina was never in doubt; Chaikin was discreetly authoritarian in his direction of the Open Theatre; and Schechner has since acknowledged the tendency himself, with regret for its consequences in avant-garde theatre. But a distinction also needs to be drawn between the *coordination* of nonetheless still distinct creative functions in a unified artistic endeavour as practised by the Open Theatre, and the essential *collapse* of these functions that occurs at the limit of collective creation, the textless, improvisatory events best represented in the Living Theatre's *Mysteries and Smaller Pieces* (1964) and *Paradise Now* (1968).This is a distinction between holistic and monistic practice, and again the benefits of the former prove illusory in the latter. In *Paradise Now* there was no script. The event, which lasted upwards of four hours, was structured in some detail and that structural outline or map was provided in lieu of a programme. It detailed eight stages of revolution, each comprising a rite, a vision and an action leading to the next level. The play begins with actors moving among the audience, whispering a series of plaints: "I'm not allowed to travel without a passport"; "I don't know how to stop the war"; "You can't live if you don't have money"; "I'm not allowed to smoke marijuana". Each one swells in crescendo to a howl. Finally, with the cry "I am not allowed to take off my clothes", the company does so, and all congregate semi-naked on the stage; members of the audience often joined them. As the play proceeds, rites and visions such as "The Vision of the Death and Resurrection of the American Indian" (in which the company form into a spectacular pyramid), and "The Rite of Universal Intercourse" (in which actors and audience join in a "love pile" onstage, writhing and anonymously caressing anyone within reach), alternate with often protracted debates and confrontations between actors and audience. The event culminates in a procession out of the theatre into the street.

Within this framework is left enormous scope for improvisation, so that the performance is itself the process of creation each time. This absence of fixed form is thoroughly integrated into the intentions behind the piece, as Beck makes clear: "We said in preparing *Paradise Now* that we wanted to make a play which would no longer be enactment but would be the act itself, that we would not reproduce something but we would try to create an event in which we would always ourselves be experiencing it, not anew at all but something else each time". [10] The Living Theatre's procedure in *Paradise Now* conflates the duality of creation and performance, for the fundamental reason that the performance, as an incitement to anarcho-pacifist revolution, cannot be a reenactment but must be "the act itself". The words "collective creation" at the bottom of the chart provided for *Paradise Now* referred not to some extant piece, but to the *process* of the evening's event, and included whatever contributions the audience themselves could provide. But there remains an element of self-deception in the aspiration of the actors to experience "something else each time". The alternative Beck rejects, to experience the event *anew* each time, is the form of scripted performance: there is a tension between the general prescription and the specific realization. In an improvised context, no such tension exists: each occasion is at liberty to define itself entire. The only possible outcome of such an open creative role, and one the Living Theatre were repeatedly found guilty of accepting, is rigidification: an inevitable slide into formula and closing down of possibilities. This applied not only to the options pursued by the actors themselves, but also to the responses they were willing to accept from the audience, so that the apparent openness came increasingly to mask an underlying coercion. At the Open

Theatre, actor's improvisations were as fundamental to the creative process, but they never became a performance strategy. Whereas spontaneity more often than not reverts to conventional formulae, an essential stage in the creative process adopted by the Open Theatre was the weeding out of cliche responses, working through the banalities of improvisation in order to reach its more profound and substantial core. Collapsing the distinction between creation and performance elided the critical reciprocity of this stage of their interaction.

The Performance Group were reprimanded by Grotowski for a similar transgression when they included some of his actors' exercises at the beginning of *Dionysus in 69* (1968), but in fact the play had a mixed economy combining a formal text derived from Euripides' *Bacchae* with improvisatory actions among the actors and between actors and audience. Its most important feature was its engagement with the dualisms of performers and audience, stage and auditorium. An "environmental", a theatrical environment embracing the whole performance site, was designed for the play by Michael Kirby and Jerry Rojo: it consisted of a complex of scaffolds, planks, ladders and platforms upon which the actors cavorted and the audience found what vantage points they could. The audience were allowed into the theatre space one at a time, while the actors performed their acrobatic exercises all around. On Grotowski's advice, parts of the play were performed naked: such was the first scene, the Birth Ritual, in which Dionysus, having introduced himself both as Dionysus and as the actor playing the part, is passed through a birth canal formed from the bodies of five men lying face down, bestridden by four women. Dionysus emerges from between the women's legs and invites the audience to participate in a celebration of his nativity. There commences a ritualized orgy in which the actors simulate sexual encounters with members of the audience, many of whom participated in the revels. Pentheus, King of Thebes, appears as a conservative figure who is both repulsed and attracted by the proceedings. He confronts Dionysus, but is mocked and humiliated by the Bacchantes, and compelled (offstage) to perform fellatio upon Dionysus. He is then condemned to die, and the women, their hands dipped in red paint, alternately caress and claw him to death. The actors then step out of role, wash the "blood" from their bodies and get dressed, while Dionysus, from the top of one of the towers, announces his candidacy for President and showers the audience with "Dionysus in 69" buttons.

In its environmental incorporation of the audience into the performance space and its powerful appeal to audience participation the play was a notable success. At the same time, it raised some of the fundamental problems in the concept of audience involvement, problems which generated resonances with the exploration of "the

politics of ecstasy" that defined the play's thematic structure. The
argument of the play, as illustrated in the brutal murder of Pentheus,
was that the ecstasy of liberation can be quickly transformed into
tyranny. At the same time, the group clearly aligned themselves with
Dionysus against the reactionary Pentheus. The group's interactions
with the audience, mainly on a physical and sexual level, were
simulated but designed to break down the distinction between feigned
and real response. Having elicited such responses, the group found
themselves drawn by the logic of the situation into one of two equally
undesired scenarios, as Stefan Brecht argued in his contemporary
analysis of the play: if the action concerned goes on to suppress the
sexuality and aggression it has aroused, "we have a conservative
society or theatre. If it stimulates and uses them, a fascist society or
theatre". [11]

The Living Theatre were the most comprehensive proponents of
interaction between audience and performers, particularly in *Mysteries*
and *Paradise Now*. *Mysteries* opens with a single actor standing silent and
impassive onstage. There he remains until the audience are provoked
to action. This was usually confined to a predictable range of jibes and
a certain amount of debate within the audience over what they were
or were not entitled to expect from a trip to the theatre. The important
point is that a degree of hostility was generated, for it was this hostility
upon which the Living Theatre's performance fed. In this they
adhered closely to the precepts of their mentor Artaud and his
"Theatre of Cruelty" – the performance is a violent therapy for the
illness of contemporary humanity, a drawing out of the "plague" by
which he signified the disharmonious split between the spiritual and
physical self. The process involves transgressing the boundaries
between stage and auditorium and a similar conflation of the roles of
(active) performer and (passive) spectator. The final scene of *Mysteries* is
an enactment of Artaud's plague, in which the group, distributed along
the aisles among the audience, perform protracted, agonized deaths
culminating in a profound *rigor mortis*. The rigid bodies are then lifted
by the neck and ankles, and stacked in layers onstage. The variations
of audience response to this scene, which the Living Theatre
performed throughout Europe as well as in America, are instructive
both in themselves and in the ways they were interpreted by the
performers. In Europe, the scene was usually understood as the
Holocaust – except in Vienna where it was apparently interpreted as
a mass orgasm. The audiences tended to participate by dying with the
performers, and those who proved sufficiently rigid corpses were lifted
and included in the funeral pile onstage. In America, by contrast, the
general audience response was to comfort the dying. Schechner, in an
interview with Beck and Malina, offered the interpretation that
"Americans don't like to participate in death. Comforting is a

sentimental act; dying is a committed act".[12] But actually the two forms of participation are different in kind. Dying with the performers constitutes a complete refutation of the dualism of actor and spectator, a form of participation that affirms a monistic community of people, audience and actors, within the theatre. Comforting the performers, on the other hand, shares the effect of a participatory community but retains a sense of separate roles, an irreducible divide between performer and spectator, *across* which this mutuality of action takes place. To die with the performers is certainly a committed act, for it implies that there is no transaction taking place between actors and audience: there is nothing to be communicated that is not already known and understood, and all that remains is to express solidarity. Malina also records a series of aggressive responses that the scene provoked on their European tour: on several occasions when she died she was kicked and tickled, had her fingers bent back and her hair set on fire; in Amsterdam the audience carried the dead out of the theatre with the intention of dropping them in a canal. Beck's understanding of this behaviour, that it was "To get the corpse not to be a real corpse"[13] is altogether too confined to the terms of the performance: these audiences had no need to prove anything so self-evident. Rather, this behaviour is a hostile, or at least mischievous message to the group that the audience are not playing; that they do not accept the terms of the performance.

These extremes of response highlight the problems raised by the Living Theatre's strategy of eliciting hostility from the audience in order to purge and sublimate it into a love compatible with their desired anarcho-pacifist revolution. These problems were exacerbated in *Paradise Now*, where the revolutionary objective was explicit and singular. Hostility proved rather more intractable than the theory required, and while it was certainly crucial to the theatrical effect of their performances, its significance as a political tool was other than that the group professed to be exploiting. While insisting upon their love for the audience, the group used oppressive and aggressively confrontational tactics. The audience's concomitantly aggressive responses resolved into either absolute dismissal or uncritical support of the group, according to the direction in which the hostility was channelled. The idea that the expression of repressed hostility leads to a moral catharsis is theoretically suspect and historically contradicted: to the extent that the Living Theatre won their audiences they were susceptible to the charge frequently levelled at them, especially in Europe, of resorting to fascist methods.

The sort of appeal to audience participation that is open to accusations of fascism is exactly that in which the consciousness that it *is* participation is lost. This loss of awareness, or simple collapse of the distinction between performer and spectator, is the critical factor which allows participation (as a collaboration aware of the difference of the collaborators) to descend into coercion. Unfortunately such a distinction was only drawn by the Open Theatre, whose use of audience participation showed a suspicion of the authoritarianism implied in generating actual physical responses, and extended no further than the distribution of apples after Eve's temptation in *The Serpent*. Both the Living Theatre and the Performance Group, on the other hand, were committed to full involvement of the audience, and adopted the means best able to achieve it – forms of direct physical and especially sexual interaction in which the distinction between a participatory role and direct personal involvement is most difficult to sustain. There are numerous recorded examples of the response of the audience at these performances exceeding the bounds of the cast's toleration, and of the attentions of the actors exceeding the toleration of members of the audience. The Living Theatre were notorious for the psychological and physical harassment to which they could subject any member of their audiences whom they suspected of opinions incompatible with their own. Their invocation of "free theatre" in *Paradise Now*, when the group and many of the audience were often high on drugs and the fraught atmosphere, produced reports of violent confrontations and even allegations of rape.

During the "caress" in *Dionysus in 69*, female members of the cast were vulnerable to the abuses of opportunistic men in the audience, who were regularly guilty of a cynical exploitation of the circumstances. But to the extent that these performances collapsed the distinction between role play and direct personal participation, how could such abuses actually constitute a cynical exploitation of the circumstances? The limit case of audience participation is a monistic model of the theatre environment in which the distinction between real behaviour and performance has broken down. This result was actively pursued by proponents of environmental theatre in spite of the complications. Schechner puts just this case when he addresses the problem of conflict between actors and audience arising out of the collapse of the defined territories of stage and auditorium into a single space: "Such conflicts have to be coped with in terms of the performance. They can be turned to a capital advantage if one believes that the interaction between performers and audience is a real and valuable one".[14] The opportunity for a "capital advantage" – the dividend of a holistic treatment of the terms "performers" and "audience" – is based on what turns out to be a monistic conflation of the ideas of the "terms of the *performance*" and a "*real* and valuable" interaction. Schechner records performances of *Dionysus in 69* during which members of the audience had to be restrained from responses to the "caress" deemed to be beyond the "terms of the performance". But when Pentheus attempts to make love to a randomly selected member of the audience, the play itself is built upon the assumption that, at some point, he will exceed the mandate of performance and be repulsed.

If incitements to audience participation succeed in collapsing the distinction between performance and actual involvement, then, its apologists equivocate as to the status of the newly formed whole. But in fact the aesthetic distance between involvement and performance is rarely confounded, and certainly not in the case of those members of the audience who seek to exploit their apparent contiguity. The participation of intelligent audiences remains role play because it is not *naive* participation: it is not the child's cry of "Behind you!" or the bumpkin's advice to Hamlet. The participation of a more sophisticated theatre-goer will always retain a sense of doubleness – as the adoption not simply of a performing role, but of the role of performer. It involves a transcendent perspective, in other words, in which the distinction between spectator and participant remains intact; and the tension between these poles is fundamental to the experience.

Implicit in all these experiments with audience involvement is an attack upon the most fundamental dualism addressed by these groups: that of the categories of theatre and life. The attempt to transcend or subvert that dualism embraces all the more specific applications of holistic methodology so far considered, and is itself symptomatic of the extraordinary presence of theatre and its forms in the countercultural life of the sixties. The Living Theatre was the group most fully committed to subverting the opposition between theatre and life, propounding instead an anti-art aesthetic which rejected the duplicity of representation, stigmatized as "illusion". Their express objective was to overcome the intrinsic absence in representational theatre by presenting instead the plenitude of theatre as pure *event*, wholly actual and present to the participants. Membership of the Living Theatre, who lived and worked as a commune, was always likely to involve arrest and periods of imprisonment for offences such as non-payment of taxes or public indecency, and prolonged periods of personal privation such as the group endured on their European tour. Political commitment therefore always took precedence over artistic criteria in the group's definition of their theatrical objectives.

The solution was to equate artistic functions with personal qualities, and reached fruition in *Paradise Now*. The rationale for *Paradise Now* was that the performance was itself an event in which the audience, led by the actors, are actually drawn towards the paradise of permanent anarcho-pacifist revolution. For such an objective to make sense, there could be no barrier between theatre and life, no point at which the revolution is abandoned as a role temporarily explored before returning to everyday reality. Malina explains how the group proposed to ensure the continuity of the performance with the world beyond it:

"Anything I say to you in the lobby is very much part of the play. If *Paradise Now* can be said to have a direction, it is that I don't have to put on any kind of an act ... But it means that if I'm talking to you in the lobby I should have what used to be called a super-objective, taking whatever we're talking about into the level of what Paradise is as far as I can at that moment".[15] The actors, then, personally enact the continuity between art and life as it operates in their own lives – in that the orientation towards their concept of Paradise does indeed run through both their personal convictions and their theatrical performance. But Malina's vacillation between presenting this continuity as "not putting on any kind of an act" and as "very much part of the play" suggests a residual concept of the division of art and life in even this most committed of theatrical events. *Paradise Now* was originally designed to end with the actors leading the audience out into the street to carry the revolution to the community. When this happened at the end of their first performance in America at Yale, several members of the group including Beck and Malina were promptly arrested for indecency. They were constrained, on pain of further arrests, to accept an undertaking not to accompany the audience beyond the confines of the theatre in subsequent performances. The New Haven Chief of Police commented, "As far as we're concerned, art stops at the door of the theater, and then we apply community standards".[16] The Living Theatre complied.

Nonetheless there remained a general commitment among these theatre groups to an idea of theatre that was not defined by the representational dualism of art and life. The primary influence was Artaud, whose own commitment in *The Theatre and its Double* was to a theory in which, "between life and the theatre there will be no distinct division, but instead a continuity".[17] Language in particular imposes a tyranny of representation upon the theatre, and Artaud's theory involved a reaction against the rupture "between things and the ideas and signs that are their representation".[18] He proposed that words should be used for their sensual qualities, the shape and sound of their articulation, their physical rather than just their signifying properties. All three groups experimented with language as pure sound, deforming its signifying function by chanting, wailing, and elongating and fragmenting its syllables. But suspicion of language ran deepest in the Open Theatre, fuelled by the flagrant abuse and manipulation of language in politics and the media and by the inadequacy of words to accurately communicate the personal explorations of the group's acting exercises. In fact the Open Theatre's actors' exercises were originally conceived as a means of "getting away from talking", and included experiments in breathing rhythm and wordless voice that were designed to explore its non-signifying properties. The ultimate objective was never to reject language completely, however, but to redefine its function in theatre. Chaikin, and for that matter Artaud, proposed that language in the theatre should be utilized for its substance, the physical facts of speech, *as well as* its meaning.

Despite its suspicion of audience participation, the Open Theatre shared in the aspiration to a theatre beyond the representational dualism of art and life. But their formulation of it, as expressed by Chaikin, was significantly different: "The theater, insofar as people are serious in it, seems to be looking for a place where it is not a duplication of life. It exists not just to make a mirror of life, but to represent a kind of realm just as certainly as music is a realm". Here the division between theatre and life is to be superseded by a third "realm" which, like music, possesses its own unique qualities. Chaikin goes on, "But because the theater involves behaviour and language, it can't be completely separate from the situational world, as music can".[19] This realm must be transcendent, rather than autonomous, because its media, unlike the medium of music, are inherently representational. To the extent that performance theatre succeeded in holding the dualism of representation and presence in suspension, it generated a dynamic reciprocity between the two which is absent from much conventional theatre. To the extent that it collapsed the opposition and offered itself as pure presence in its enthusiasm for the immediacy of the event, it lost that depth – and in the process lost consciousness.

Political Orientations

In a sense any form of protest constitutes an attack on prevailing dualisms: inequality between races, classes, genders or sexual orientations is the prioritizing of a normative group, just as the privileged interests of such a group rationalize internal policing and foreign wars. To agitate against some aspect of this prioritization is to deny the validity of the hierarchical dualism it implies: the tendency is to assert instead a holistic equivalence of its terms. Such was the nature of the civil rights movement in the fifties and early sixties under the dominant influence of the Southern Christian Leadership Conference and non-violent direct action. The main theme was desegregation, its form moral reprehension. In the theatre it was most notably articulated in Loraine Hansberry's *A Raisin in the Sun* (1959), which confronted Broadway audiences with the prejudice by which the integration of a black family into American middle class life is prohibited. Five years later Amiri Baraka (then LeRoi Jones) advanced a very different argument in *Dutchman* and *The Slave*, marking a transition in the politics of black Americans that can be related to a more general transformation in the politics and theatre of protest in the period. In *Dutchman*, the middle-class assimilationist Clay is baited on a subway by a sexually provocative white woman, Lola. Clay warns that the alternative to his assimilationism is violence, but is himself stabbed by Lola. The passengers drag him from the train, and the play ends as another young black enters the compartment. The protagonist of *The Slave*, Walker Vessels, confronts his white ex-wife and her liberal husband Easley in an effort to liberate himself from his assimilationist past. Vessels is accused of inverted racism (a charge he does not answer), and goes on to kill Easley. But as Easley himself makes explicit, this is ritual drama: Vessels' act is an individual rite of passage, violence a repudiation of the alternative ritual to which Clay is sacrificed.

The shift from integration to militant separatism and black power was a realization that equality could never arise from black assimilation to a social order defined by whites. This was an illusory holism, its collapse of racial dualisms actually producing a monistic social order in which white culture would remain irreducibly proprietary. The value of the civil rights movement was to be seen not in its victories over segregation, but in its demonstration of the possibility of a specifically black empowerment: the pursuit of equal entitlement to universal values was superseded by an anti-monistic assertion of racially specific values. In the theatre, while the Negro Ensemble Company played to integrated audiences, Baraka's Black Arts Repertory Theatre in Harlem affirmed a nascent cultural nationalism by addressing itself exclusively to blacks. Baraka's *The Baptism* and *The Toilet*, (also produced in 1964, but originating in his Greenwich Village bohemian phase) were cast in universal thematic and aesthetic terms: their preoccupations are personal identity and development, appearance and reality. They engage in social analysis, exploring the conflicting demands of society upon the individual, but they are not racial plays. His shift to cultural nationalism is a recognition that the "universal" is already culturally defined, is in fact an exclusive category operating to marginalize cultural elements alien to the dominant culture. Although the line between cultural nationalism and inverted racism was sometimes blurred in the rhetoric of black power, the conceptual distinction is plain: the objective is not to invert the monism of establishment culture, but to subvert it by consolidating black cultural solidarity. Such is the orientation of Baraka's *Slave Ship* (1967), which exploits the form of an Afro-American historical pageant to maximize its argument for the continuity of a specifically black sense of cultural identity. It is notably the Uncle Tom figure, the black who identifies with the dominant culture and so betrays the interests of his race, who is singled out as the enemy throughout history. To some extent Baraka's later repudiation of cultural nationalism in favour of communism can be interpreted as a progression beyond anti-monism to the pursuit of a transcendent holism cast in terms of economic equality. Certainly it involved the rejection of much of his earlier work as chauvinistic, and in plays like *S-1* (1976), this redefined fight against the capitalist regime produced a previously unthinkable appeal to the assimilationist middle class, now seen as merely lackeys of the system, equally deprived of the means of production. But more probably the economic criteria have here simply obliterated all other distinctions, instituting a new revolutionary monism: the absence of dialectic in the plays would tend to suggest this latter interpretation.

Ed Bullins, strongly influenced by Baraka, was an outspoken advocate of black power, and briefly Cultural Minister for the Black Panther Party. In his *The Gentleman Caller* (1969), a black working-class maid forcibly educates the middle-class male protagonist about the falseness of the white values that have seduced him by killing the rich mistress who embodies them. It is a parable, its ritual aspect showing the influence of *Dutchman* and *The Slave*. Even the plays of his "Twentieth Century Cycle", beginning with *In the Wine Time* (1968), insist upon metaphoric interpretation in their framing and disrupting of naturalistic features, and make cultural signifiers of the everyday rituals of black life around which they revolve. Cultural nationalism is pervasive in Bullin's plays, but with a critical awareness that is absent from Baraka's work after 1964. *Dialect Determinism* (1965), for example, satirizes revolutionary ideologues, its messianic "Boss Brother" evolving through a series of demagogic roles to end as an eager martyr to nationalism. Bullins resists the foreclosure of debate characteristic of agit-prop even when he most imitates the form: in *Death List* (1970), a revolutionary cleans his gun while reciting a list of black leaders who are traitors to black solidarity; but at the same time a woman harangues him, denying his authority, suggesting extenuating circumstances, questioning the outcome of violence. The play ends with the revolutionary offstage and the sound of a single shot: it has the function of a question. Within this interrogative context, however, his anti-assimilationism remains constant. In *The Taking of Miss Janie* (1975), inter-racial rape becomes a symbol of the impossible relationship between blacks and white liberals, the inevitable repudiation of a patronizing friendship that could only consolidate the forms of oppression.

Given the frequency with which black separatism exploited the imagery of sexual aggression, black women had a difficult relationship to the feminist debate that began to gather momentum towards the end of the sixties. Being doubly marginalized, black women have a particular insight into the confusion of dualistic, monistic and holistic ideological frameworks. Adrienne Kennedy's *Funnyhouse of a Negro*

(1964) established the traumatized psychological terrain over which the contradictory claims of racial identity and sexual identity fragment the black woman, locating her only resolution in death. As black cultural nationalism and subsequently radical feminism sought to consolidate and affirm the marginalized identities of blacks and women, rejecting the bogus monistic unity of integrationist politics, the black woman encountered a secondary monism perpetuating her oppression *within* each of these groups. The black feminist debate was energized by Ntozake Shange's *For colored girls who have considered suicide/ when the rainbow is enuf* (1975), in which the painful emergence of self-worth in black women is wrested from the oppressions even of language and logic in dance and poem collage. The interference of dimensions of marginality that characterize the black woman's position leaves no unified site on which to build an identity: instead it must be done on the run (or in a dance), in the gaps of syntax and logical schemata. But this same irreducibly plural identity positively contributes to the suspension of discrete elements in unity that characterizes a genuinely holistic perspective, and forbids any relapse into covertly monistic forms. This potential has to a degree informed feminist discourse in general, and feminist theatre has benefitted from its belatedness among the radical theatres of the period.

The first explicitly feminist theatre in America was established by Anselma dell'Olio in 1969: the New Feminist Theatre addressed feminist issues directly and powerfully within the clearly defined limits of a conventional theatrical structure and aesthetic, and liberal feminist arguments. Indicative was their production of Myrna Lamb's *But What Have You Done for Me Lately?* (1969), in which a man implanted with a uterus is subjected to the trauma of unwanted pregnancy. The polemical thrust of this role reversal, its "how would you like it?" rhetoric, implies both its address to an establishment audience and its liberal focus upon the double standards oppressing women. Dell'Olio retained personal authority as a director, and although she went on to produce feminist theatre within a more adventurous aesthetic context in her improvisational *Cabaret of Sexual Politics*, she continued to seek establishment audiences and resisted the affirmation of any particularized womanhood in her desire for "universality". The suspicion that this universality in itself deferred to the forms of patriarchy, and that liberal feminism in general aspired no higher than a dubious immanent holism, led to the emergence of a theatre dedicated to an anti-monistic radical feminism.

It's All Right to Be Woman Theatre, formed in 1970, were a radical feminist collective who rejected the hierarchical group structure retained by dell'Olio as implicitly patriarchal, and instituted an affirmative separatism by restricting their audiences to women only. Their performances originated in improvisations around life material supplied by members of the group, and in performance they retained this orientation towards the expression of feelings rather than theatrical statement. Often this improvisational technique would be explored further in performance, the actors miming dream narratives volunteered by one of the group or a member of the audience. Such an approach was firmly grounded in the methodology of consciousness-raising, developed by Kathie Sarachild and widely adopted as a radical feminist strategy for propagating solidarity and enabling participants to become "woman-identified". The concept was extended by the Minneapolis group, At the Foot of the Mountain Theatre, in their 1976 production, *Raped*: the performers interrupted the play with documentary rape testimonies, elevating it to a "ritual drama" in which the audience were also encouraged to participate.

The same radicalization of sexual politics prompted many of the preeminent women in avant-garde theatre to make a decisive break in their careers: Roberta Sklar left the Open Theatre after *The Mutation Show* to form the Women's Experimental Theatre; Megan Terry abandoned New York to establish the Omaha Magic Theatre; Martha Kearns left the Bread and Puppet Theatre for the Wilma Theatre. Radical feminist theatre appropriated much of the current experimentation of performance theatre to a specifically female aesthetic: groups like the Women's Experimental Theatre and At the Foot of the Mountain made their plays non-linear, resisted the authority of narrative closure, used documentary style and addressed their audiences directly. The prevalence of these techniques, as well as the importance of consciousness-raising (and its performance equivalents, audience participation and discussion) indicates a concerted effort to subvert the dualisms of art and life, performers and audience. But this underlying holism within the anti-monistic context of radical feminism easily reverts to the forms against which such groups had reacted: the assertion and consolidation of difference tended towards a simple inversion of received gender polarities, and the consequent advocacy of a counter-universalism. Such tendencies are apparent in the way the assertion of female gender values gravitated towards an essentialist concept of "Woman", the most obvious aesthetic manifestation of which is the advancement of *l'écriture féminine* and its associated discursive forms. While radical feminist essentialism was embraced in the context of an urgent political need to affirm sexual difference, it elided any differences that threatened the integrity of womanhood: differences of race, and of sexuality. Feminist separatism led to a politicized idea of lesbianism, but sublimated as female bonding and woman-identification: lesbian sexuality itself was a threat to the homogeneity of womanhood, introducing a multiplicity of sexual roles. More recently, lesbian theatre such as that centred upon the WOW Café in New York has used just this availability of multiple sexual roles to move beyond radical feminist ideology. Instead of a concept of the female as defined by sexual difference (which remains subordinate to the patriarchal dualism and so abets its mode of gender representation) they enact the female as the site of differences. Performers and audience participate in a foregrounding of culturally constructed gender roles by parading the interchangeability of "butch" and "femme" lesbian roles, generating a theatrical context in which femininity itself is represented as drag. This presents gender as a rigorously holistic site that recognizes the interference of sexual, racial, economic and cultural differences and by denaturalizing them, denies any essentialist concept of identity: it foregrounds the enculturation of gender by showing its polarities in competition with others in the construction of subjectivity.

Gay theatre, and more particularly the "Theatre of the Ridiculous", has also made vital use of the affirmation of role in its sexual politics – not that politics as such is manifested in a theatre whose fundamental aesthetic orientation, camp, is an absolute refusal of anything so earnest. The catalyst for this theatre was Jack Smith, whose pop art films *Flaming Creatures* and *Normal Love* established the most salient features of its sensibility: a spirit of travesty and the celebration of bad taste, sexual ambiguity and eroticism, and an extravagant flamboyance of manner. The Playhouse of the Ridiculous was established by John Vaccaro and Ronald Tavel in 1966, their first play being *The Life of Lady Godiva*. In their brief collaboration, Tavel and Vaccaro created a theatre in which contradiction and paradox were constitutive. It nihilistically exposed the pretensions of a humanity conceived of as irredeemably low, sordid and ridiculous, camping the ultimate illusion of love in an avowedly amoral burlesque. At the same time, it sustained a perversely ethical commitment to truth in its refusal of redemptive illusion; its insistence upon universal artifice propagated a resilient aestheticism, a real aspiration towards the beauty it seemed to deny; and out of this emerged an illicit sense of tragedy. Tavel left in 1967 and Charles Ludlam, who had been an actor in the group, became its new playwright. After two productions (*Big Hotel* and *Conquest of the Universe*), Ludlam also split with Vaccaro to found the Ridiculous Theatrical Company and launch a new production of the latter play under the title When *Queens Collide*. Vaccaro's apparent talent for volatile collaboration was further manifested with the introduction of Kenneth Bernard, whose talents, particularly in *The Moke-Eater* (1968) and *Night Club* (1970), brought a nightmarish grotesque to the Ridiculous vision.

The camp sensibility has been well articulated by Susan Sontag, who tempers her appreciation of it with misgivings about its refusal of political engagement. But to withdraw so ostentatiously from the political arena is in itself a very political act, and equates directly with the rejection of condescending assimilation as a political goal by black nationalism and radical feminism. The nurturing of a camp sensibility is a far-reaching affirmation of difference, and the sexual role-play of transvestism and androgyny in which it delights compares with the feminist theatre's redemption of sexuality from the binary opposition of biological gender. Charles Ludlam has identified the political significance of the Ridiculous theatre in just such terms: "Politics is about spheres of influence, and in that sense it is political. If a man plays Camille, for instance, you begin to think it's horrible, but in the end you are either moved or won over. You believe in the character beyond the gender of the actor, and no one who has experienced that can go back.[20]

There is no question of disengagement in the Chicano theatre of Luis Valdez, established in Delano, California in 1965 explicitly to support the strike of Chicano field workers and the struggle to establish a farmworkers' union. El Teatro Campesino recruited performers from among the workers themselves and their performances, usually given from the flatbed of a truck, were aimed unambiguously at sustaining the morale and political commitment of the strikers. Their "actos" relied upon broad comedy – slapstick, impersonations – and the use of stereotypes as the vehicle of political satire. Actors performed with signs around their necks designating them as Huelgista (striker), Patroncito (grower), Esquirol (strikebreaker/scab), and Contratista (contractor). The Teatro's immersion in the community it served made audience participation intrinsic to its aesthetic in a pre-theatrical way it could never be for the East Coast performance groups: this interactive solidarity is the characteristic vehicle of an anti-monistic, oppositional definition of interests. The actos are particularly concerned to resist any pernicious assimilation to the ideological perspective of the growers: in *Las dos caras del patroncito* (The Two Faces of the Boss, 1965) the Esquirol is deluded into a subservient alliance with the Patroncito – whose mask he takes on. In *Vietnam Campesino* (1970), the Campesinos are shown to have more in common with the Vietnamese peasants than with the Anglos and the military who conspire to oppress them both. The very specific solidarity of the Campesinos took on larger cultural implications for the Chicanos, and an emergent cultural nationalism began to inform the plays. Stereotypes, functioning to define the strikers oppositionally, were supplemented by archetypes serving to reconnect the Chicanos to their cultural heritage. Alongside the actos the Teatro developed the corridos, stylized dramatizations of Mexican ballads, and the mitos, in which contemporary events were represented through ritual, legend and myths that located Chicano culture in a context of Aztec mythology and Mayan philosophy. In 1970, Valdez established El Centro Campesino Cultural as a collective dedicated to the promotion of Chicano cultural nationalism and the celebration of the barrio. But at the same time, the Teatro Campesino maintained a sense of the multiplicity of Chicano identity. The very fact of language guaranteed the prominence of this condition from the earliest actos: they moved freely between Spanish and English, accommodating non-English speakers through the transparency of their meaning and the extensive use of mime. Valdez took the syncretism by which Chicano culture contains both its pre-Columbian and Christian heritages as a defining characteristic, finding parallels between the doubleness of the Mexican-American and that enshrined within Mexican culture itself, in the system of Indian mythology. So the figure of Quetzalcoatl and the symbol of the Plumed Serpent come to express the possibility of a holistic reconciliation of the diverse elements of Chicano culture. Nor does this philosophy remain marginalized within that context: *Zoot Suit*, described by Valdez as an "American play", reached Broadway in 1979. Valdez has since become involved in the film industry, the 1982 movie of *Zoot Suit* being a deliberate "mainstreaming" of his concept of Chicano cultural integrity in the furtherance of a holistic multiculturalism in American society at large.

Before forming El Teatro Campesino, Valdez had been briefly a member of the San Francisco Mime Troupe, and had taken with him their concern with mime and commedia dell'arte techniques. The San Francisco Mime Troupe was founded by R.G. Davis in 1959, initially to explore the avant-garde possibilities of mime. The shift to commedia which began with *The Dowry* (1961) accompanied a movement out into the parks of San Francisco and the need to attract popular interest. Commedia techniques, the use of stock characters defined by masks and set piece situations allowing improvisational comedy and visual jokes (all drawing upon the foundations of the group's background in mime) enabled the group to draw a crowd, sustain their attention and respond flexibly to the performance situation. Civil rights issues, Vietnam and repeated clashes with the authorities radicalized the group through the sixties, and their performance techniques were turned to political use in such plays as *A Minstrel Show, or Civil Rights in a Cracker Barrel* (1965), which addressed racial oppression in Watts in anticipation of the riots there. In *L'Amant Militaire* (1967), Joan Holden adapted Goldoni to the needs of anti-Vietnam protest, at the same time taking the group beyond its pacifist assumptions towards active resistance. Accompanying this radicalization was a shift in the dynamics of the group itself, and Davis's loss of authority led to his departure in 1970. The group subsequently became a collective, adopting an increasingly agit-prop stance in its attempts to reach a working-class audience. Instrumental in the split with Davis was an emergent feminist resistance to the patriarchal structure of the group, and their first post-Davis play, *The*

Independent Female, or A Man Has His Pride (1970), articulated this concern in its attack upon male chauvinism; it also marked a further shift towards identification with popular audiences by replacing the stylistic framework of commedia with native melodrama. The group became committed to collective creation, producing didactic pieces on the methodology of subversion such as *Meter Maid* and *Ripping Off Ma Bell* (1970), and a further satire of Vietnam, *The Dragon Lady's Revenge* (1971), which implicated the CIA in the Indo-China heroin trade. The group dedicated itself increasingly to the objective of political mobilization, explicitly conflating art and politics and regarding theatre as an articulation of political community, while Davis went into print to register his dissent from the group's post-1970 orientations. Davis's objections and the group's responses as articulated by Joan Holden centre upon several aspects of the relation between political theatre and holistic principles. Davis was distressed by the loss of dialectics resulting from the group's increasing didacticism, distinguishing sharply between their earlier *political* theatre, which retained an investigative function, and their later agit-prop, which merely supported an established agenda. Holden points out that *The Independent Female* was drastically revised after discussion with a committed feminist audience in which the play was severely criticized. But this illustration of the group's continuing openness to political debate is extrinsic to their art, and in fact the criticism centred upon the way the play's parody of melodrama tended to undermine its feminist message. In accepting the criticism, the group resolved the dualism of art and politics in favour of a monistic suppression of art. The issue of collective creation turned upon the same argument: Davis felt that it could only be a dissolution of specialized talents, the agent of a homogenizing mediocrity in the name of equality. Holden insisted that it did not function in this way, that it implied a levelling not of talents but of power relations: the process did not involve collectivized creative roles but, precisely, a system of "checks and balances".[21] This appears to be a valid holistic framework, but it is vitiated by the fate of her own script for *The Independent Female*; and T*he Dragon Lady's Revenge*, which had five writers, was stylistically fragmentary in consequence. Ultimately, artistic criteria were not balanced by political imperatives, but checked.

Probably the theatre group most associated with protest against the Vietnam war was Peter Schumann's Bread and Puppet Theatre, whose giant puppets paraded at many of the era's marches and demonstrations. In the Bread and Puppet Theatre the developments of the aesthetic and political avant-gardes were most fully integrated, and for that reason its relationship to the competing frameworks of monistic, anti-monistic and holistic principles was exceptionally complex. It was founded in 1962, the name expressing Schumann's

belief that "theatre should be as basic as bread",[22] that theatre should
feed the mind just as the bread passed round by the group after
performances fed the body. The Christian imagery expresses
Schumann's religious concept of art, its function as the framework for
communality that religion once was, and indicates the group's
ambiguously holistic aspirations. In combination with (and perhaps
opposition to) the theatre's bread were its puppets: Schumann
experimented a great deal with puppets and masks, from plaster face
casts and skull masks to giant caricature figures like the "Shark Plane"
and "Uncle Fatso" (instantly identified with Johnson); from Japanese
Bunraku puppets to the sad, wise oriental faces and huge expressive
hands of the "Gray Ladies". Schumann has said that "alienation is
automatic with puppets",[23] and their aesthetic importance was
fundamentally Brechtian. The group's puppeteers generally worked in
clear view of the audience, sharing with and exemplifying for them a
critical distance from the puppets they manipulated. In the sixties the
puppets served as vehicles for communication of a political content in
allegory, dumb show and agit-prop sketches, and the aesthetics by
which this was facilitated were the anti-monistic principles of Brechtian
dissociation, resisting the illusionist conflation of life and art, actor and
character. This dissociation ought to be assimilable to a properly
holistic perspective in which it becomes a dialectic, but the religiosity
of Schumann's art appears to have worked against it. Stefan Brecht
has shown that the group's anti-war agitation was associated with its
early liberal-pacifist, Old Left phase: and following the transition to
radical resistance with the emergence of the New Left and such
associated countercultural movements as the Yippies – the phase
which marks the political equivalent of the anti-monism of their
aesthetic – the Bread and Puppet Theatre gradually withdrew from the
centre of political action. The group's presence was greatest at the
early parades, with *Gas for Vietnam* in Washington, 1965, or *The Shark
Plane* in the 1966 Fifth Avenue Parade. Their Vietnam plays (*Fire, A
Man Says Goodbye to His Mother, Burning Towns, Johnny Comes Marching
Home*) tend to treat the war as archetypal, infused with the desire for
transcendence of Schumann's Christian mysticism. This sat uneasily
with a climate of political confrontation, and in 1970 Schumann
abandoned New York for a farm in Vermont.

   The subsequent development of Bread and Puppet was towards a
more and more inclusive concept of theatre. Schumann declared, "We
will build a circus ... and in the circus we will demonstrate the whole
world".[24] In 1975 Schumann staged a bicentennial "Domestic
Resurrection Circus" on his Vermont farm. The event included
pageants, processions, tableaux, impromptu and set piece
performances, sculpture, dance, music, songs, feasts and circus in a
festival based upon the structure of medieval mystery play cycles.

Despite the formal diversity, the impetus towards a romanticized idyll of communion was pervasive, and Schumann's holistic aesthetic seems always to translate into a monistic political idealism. An oppositional politics does remain in evidence: Schumann pointedly centred his bicentennial celebration upon the American Indian, upholding native American cultural and philosophical traditions. But even this is drawn into the prevailing dissolution of differences by an appropriation of the unifying symbolic role of the circle and the principle of oneness with the environment that characterizes American Indian philosophy. This does not function *within* opposition to serve a sustainable anti-monism, but diffuses into a generalized spirit of affirmation: it is at least questionable whether the anti-monism of political opposition is resilient enough in Schumann's theatre to prevent its overriding holistic impulse from reverting into an ideologically entropic non-differentiation.

The case of the Bread and Puppet Theatre serves to illustrate a particular dilemma of political theatre. Underlying radical political stances is the ideal of a truly holistic social structure enabling equality without oppressive conformism, whether this is articulated in cultural, economic or sexual arenas. But the expression of political radicalism is necessarily oppositional, characterized by the anti-monistic phase needed to distinguish its always deferred holistic ideals from monistic assimilation to prevailing structures. Because artistic freedom is rather less embattled than certain political freedoms, and because political opposition requires a sense of oppositional *community*, the aesthetics of radical political theatre very often share the holistic paradigm by which performance theatre sought unity with its audiences. But these holistic paradigms are themselves liable to at least two fatal distortions: to become monistic, and so repeat the power structures they purport to oppose; or to become universal, subsuming political anti-monism in an inevitably premature transcendent unity no longer capable of any opposition at all.

Aesthetic Orientations

Radical theatre provided a public forum for the activism of the sixties, but it also fostered a more private aesthetic attuned to the shift in cultural climate that placed the self at the centre of attention in the seventies. Two figures who exemplify this aesthetic orientation are Robert Wilson and Richard Foreman, both of whom established themselves in the late sixties as auteur directors exploring an intensely personal theatrical imagery. In 1968 Robert Wilson set up the Byrd Hoffman Foundation, dedicated to running workshops and giving performances in theatre, dance and related arts. Byrd Hoffman was the name of a dancer who in 1958 had helped Wilson overcome a speech impediment that had afflicted him up to the age of seventeen. The therapy, which was based on the release of tension through physical exercises, was later applied by Wilson in his own work with brain damaged children, and had a significant place in his concept of theatre and the displacement of language within it. Principles of the juxtaposition of images – both simultaneously and sequentially – operate centrally in Wilson's theatre, as in the Happenings. The plays do often have representational aspects, but these are in the service of an emphasis on the present moment of aesthetic experience. His concerns are form and rhythm, shape and sound, rather than character, plot, scene and dialogue. His performers, like those involved in Happenings, were (at least in the earlier plays) non-professionals, and appear generally as themselves, not in character.

In its visual character, Wilson's theatre is reminiscent of a masque: he uses the stage as a canvas on which complex images are constructed and presented much as in a *tableau vivant*. Wilson trained as an architect and aspired briefly to be a painter before settling upon the theatre, and he proceeds in the terms of those disciplines. The *space* of the stage is primary in his plays: the action is restricted to slow, carefully choreographed movements through the spatial order. These are frequently diagonal traverses of the constructed planes of the stage image, which is formally characterized by a perspectivist layering of visual elements. The temporal dimension of the plays is abstracted from ordinary experience by its lack of causal logic (there is no narrative coherence to their action, formal unity being located in the development of images); by the slowness of the action (performers moving with varying degrees of slow motion); and by the extraordinary length of the performances. Wilson's early plays each incorporated their predecessors, *The Life and Times of Sigmund Freud* (1969, 4½ hrs) including *The King of Spain* (1969) as its second act, and the 1971 version of *Deafman Glance* (8½ hrs) incorporating Freud as its fourth act. *The Life and Times of Joseph Stalin* (1973) included *Freud*, *Deafman Glance* and material from *Overture* (1972) and *Ka Mountain* (1972) in its seven acts, and lasted twelve hours. *Ka Mountain* itself lasted twenty-four hours in Paris, and in Iran extended over seven days. This extraordinary assault on the audience's capacities of attention is very much akin to the strategies by which the Happenings brought the powers of awareness into question, and the intended effect is the same: to make explicit the operations of awareness in the audience to the extent that this becomes itself the argument of the play, which addresses itself to its reform.

Wilson's plays make no statements, offer no nugget of meaning: they offer visions, and the *sense* that they are significant – that they are meaningful, but quite possibly the unique significations of their meaning.[25] This synonymy of the play with its significance contrasts with the dualism of referential meaning: it is an imminent holism antithetical to the functioning of language. Stefan Brecht has characterized Wilson's project as the development of a "right-brain dominated theatre",[26] structured according to the faculties associated with the right side of the brain, which is visual, intuitive, imaginative and *synthetic* in its operations. Verbal, causal, logical and analytical faculties are characteristic of the left brain, which is therefore commonly the site of language disabilities – and the attempt to create a theatre which circumvents them has direct links with the therapeutic strategies Wilson learned from Byrd Hoffman. The right brain is primarily visual, but also tactile, aural and conceptual: the common feature of its faculties is synthetic apprehension. A right-brain theatre must therefore be pre-eminently holistic, creating and apprehending wholes not by the linear accumulation of discrete units of imagery but as *gestalten*, in one. This model of theatre involves the displacement of language, and in Wilson's early plays words are used more as aural phenomena than as agents of meaning. But ultimately a holistic concept of theatrical apprehension must synthesize the right- and left-brain modes themselves. Such is the development in Wilson's theatre that began with *A Letter for Queen Victoria* (1974), in which Stefan Brecht, who was directly involved, locates a new concern to engage with linguistic meaning. For this play, as in the subsequent *$-Value of Man* (1975), Wilson used Christopher Knowles, a brain-damaged boy, as the mediator between play and audience and between modes of understanding. But in his mediation Knowles emerged as a superior-victim, accentuating rather than resolving the opposition: Wilson's attempt to incorporate language tended to be dominated by the need to subvert its authority. The tension persists through *Einstein on the Beach* (1976, his best known work, augmented by the music and lyrics of Philip Glass) and the more direct treatment of language in *I Was Sitting on My Patio This Guy Appeared I Thought I Was Hallucinating* (1977), which ironizes the structure of dialogue. The difficulty would appear to be inherent in the project of a holistic model of theatrical meaning: because of the self-reflexive turn by which Wilson's theatre addresses the very faculties that conceived it, the holistic model itself is constituted by its dualistic opposition to analytical orientations.

The link between Wilson's theatre and that of Foreman is quite close: both present an evolving series of complex images upon the stage without recourse to any logic of narrative or thematic unity, or indeed any inherent purposiveness that could imbue it with communicative intent. Both are therefore ultimately concerned with the faculties and nature of awareness. While Wilson's theatre does not present itself as a specific awareness, however, Foreman's is offered, by its contextual framing and Foreman's own presence as the orchestrator of each performance, as the documentation of his own. Foreman's proximity to Wilson is apparent in his favourable review of *The Life and Times of Sigmund Freud* in terms of the conceptual apparatus by which he explains his own theatre. Foreman contrasts Wilson's approach with the traditional concern to evoke specific emotion in response to a specific object, identifying instead "a non-manipulative aesthetic which would see art create a 'field' situation within which the spectator can examine himself (as perceptor)".[27] The role of the spectator, self-consciously formulating a response to non- or multiply-determined phenomena, is synthesized with that of the artist. The resistance to communicated meaning is also a programmatic attempt to transcend the opposition between art and life: Foreman explicitly equates the "real" with the "impenetrable". This is not to say that meaning, or at least its aura, is excluded: he describes the play's "most powerful" last act, for example, as a twentieth century nativity scene. But meaning is itself conceived of as a field, evoking a "whole *spectrum* of feeling", in which is epitomized "the freedom-bestowing aim of art".[28]

Foreman's avant-garde work has been performed under the auspices of the Ontological-Hysteric Theatre, his first play, *Angelface*, appearing in 1968. His Ontological-Hysteric style was established in *Total Recall (Sophia=(Wisdom): Part 2)* (1970), *HOTEL CHINA* (1971), *Sophia=(Wisdom) Part 3: The Cliffs* (1972), *Vertical Mobility (Sophia=(Wisdom): Part 4)* (1974) and *PAIN(T)* (1974): visually, it was characterized by an increasingly deep, narrow stage, divided into frames; strings linking props (and sometimes actors); and coloured lights, buzzers, taped dialogues and projected text multiplying the dimensions of the presentation. Foreman's premise was to break down the theatre into its elemental structure, and treat those elements – story, action, sound, light, composition, gesture – "in terms of the smallest building block units, the basic cells of the perceived experience of both living and art-making".[29] He has also termed his theatre "polyphonic", to indicate the way these elements work to fragment each other leaving the spectator "relatively free from empathy and identification".[30] The continuity with the Happenings is very evident: Foreman's art is atomized in order to assert a universality of phenomena subject to the synthetic attentions of consciousness with which he is preoccupied. Gertrude Stein was another vital influence upon his concept of theatre, in particular her distinction between "entity" writing and "identity" writing and the whole chain of oppositions it subordinates. Foreman's allegiance to entity writing is to a concept of art as a pure thing-in-itself, and so characterized by the collapse of traditional theatre's formative dualisms: it is timeless, present and immediate; a discontinuous, organic process rather than the slave of causal relations; an actuality rather than a reconstruction;

an introspective consideration of the human mind rather than the social dynamics of human nature. The continuous present of Stein's landscape plays is the space in which his work unfolds; it is also incorporated into his method of composition, which is foregrounded both in the plays themselves and in his considerable theoretical output. One such piece declares his belief in "the efficacy of false starts" – Stein's "beginning again and again" – a principle which aims at sustaining the field of possibility beyond the process of creation: "My habit is to try and write *BEFORE* writing ... through such an 'I *MIGHT*' of writing, the rest of the world of the not-written is still somehow available ...".[31] The rationale for sustaining attention to the process of creation *within* the work itself is precisely that this process is "not unique to the artist in question (myself) but typical of the building up which goes on through all modes of coming-into-being".[32] Foreman's aim is to show "how it is with us, in consciousness ... moment-by-moment", emphasizing the interaction between consciousness and reality. The general collapse of theoretical dualisms in his art serves to concentrate all dynamic tension upon this relation, which is treated holistically: he locates his plays "where event undergoes its sudden flashlike transformation into idea ... there on that level, with the process rather than before (in event) or after (in idea) ... in that place where sense arises".[33]

Behind this orientation lies a polemic against art that "tries to convince (usually in the realm of feeling)" and the imperative towards mastery it implies. Most theatre, he urges, is "subtly enslaving to those who 'make the effort' not to be bored by what they already know to be true (i.e. their own emotional responses to murders, loves, betrayals, righteous indignation in the face of injustice, and all those other fine things that classical art is always 'about')".[34] Foreman therefore chooses to locate his theatre at the point "where signification makes its choices,' and this situation, rather than the hermeneutic activity that would lead beyond it, is its ultimate goal: "The choices themselves aren't the important thing, but the being there, where everything is available, where all options are still present, that is the DELIGHT! In the MIND! Where one can laugh and be wise and free and in paradise!"[35] This is the highest reach of the holistic aspiration, as a paradise of suspended potentialities, a sort of negative capability, in which is achieved a "distribution of the self over the spread network of what is available". Implicit in such an approach to theatre is a concept of failure, of which (Foreman acknowledges) his work is itself a document. The fall from paradise is a necessary consequence of the admission that "it ALWAYS makes sense. Sense *can't* be avoided".[36] Themes, conventionally understood, do emerge. Foreman himself identifies as examples the exploration of the relation of knowing and dying to habit and convention in *Pandering to the Masses* (1975), or the urge to tumescence of "body-things" as they try to swamp mind-things in *Rhoda in Potatoland* (1975). But more fundamentally, there is a self-reflexiveness in Foreman's project which must necessarily displace its principles into products: "the writing is generated in a certain way which ends up producing structures with a form and texture which is the very embodiment of the theories and goals which are the 'reasons for doing the writing'". [37] Accordingly, the resistance to "mastery", to the delineation of specific meaning, becomes in itself "the meaning". Commenting on his use of disjunction to resist unified meaning by actively engaging the spectator within a polysemic field, he says: "To create that field (rather than allowing the consciousness to be hypnotized) my plays keep 'changing the subject.' But is it changed? Since the subject is the field …". [38] As a record of the impossibility of its own aspirations, Foreman's theatre is a compelling example of the paralysis of endless self-transcendence induced by a holistic impulse turned inward.

In 1981, Richard Schechner published an important two-part essay entitled "The Decline and Fall of the (American) Avant-Garde". The essay provoked a vociferous response, to the effect that the avant-garde was very far from in decline. Perhaps Schechner's title was wrong: what he does describe, with a clear awareness of his own share of the responsibility, is the demise of the holistic aspirations that animated radical theatre in the sixties and seventies. Taking the issue of creative control as his benchmark, he acknowledges a wilful confusion on the part of directors between holistic collective creation and an individualistic appropriation of the creative authority of writers. This paradigm of the individualist canker within communitarianism underlies the decline of performance theatre into the "extreme personalism" of autobiographical solo performance; the increasing marginalization of the theatre as a political forum and model of community; and the introversion of theatrical aesthetics in the apotheosis of subjectivity. But Schechner recognizes, in his own terms, the abused distinction at the root of these transformations: "A director is concerned with the holistic nature of the production … It's much different to make a part into the whole than to make a whole from many parts". [39]

Even supposing a decline in radical theatre, at least in terms of the number of significant groups and their level of activity, its worth cannot be measured without considering its relation to the mainstream in American theatre. Sam Shepard, for example, emerged as a major playwright directly out of the avant-garde environment of off-off-Broadway. He was closely associated with the Open Theatre, and has since collaborated with Joseph Chaikin in *Tongues* (1978) and *Savage/Love* (1979). His ironic view of the Happenings and the radical belief in performance as event-in-itself does not diminish the clear parallels in his own work, in which character, action, dialogue are not representational but presented, as material for the engagement of the imagination. His plays are explorations of consciousness – his own, as his frequently personal imagery indicates, but also his audiences', invoked in the process of imposing coherence upon the fields of his symbolic play. This form of audience relation also constitutes his qualification of the more overt strategies of audience involvement practised by performance theatre groups (which was the issue at the centre of his disagreement with Richard Schechner over the Performance Group's production of *The Tooth of Crime* in 1973). Again, his concern with language as sound, with its rhythms and with its force as incantation, is recognizably related to the radical theatre's explorations in language. In this respect David Mamet, by now equally canonical, might be invoked. Mamet's metatheatrical preoccupations in *A Life in the Theatre* (1976), which played with the ubiquity of role and performance, responds to (and inverts) the radical theatre's fundamental insistence upon various forms of the conflation of theatre with life; but a more specific connection may be found in his attitude to language. The naturalistic aura of Mamet's dialogue should not obscure the fact that he is vitally concerned with language in its own right, and in particular with aspects of its opacity to communication – the same emphasis upon the non-signifying surface that had preoccupied the avant-garde. Mamet's use of language often subordinates the advancement of the dialogue to essentially musical criteria, especially in such early plays as *Duck Variations* (1972). The opaque surface of language, divorced from its referents, serves as a defence against problematic emotions in *Sexual Perversity in Chicago* (1974); it furthers the transposition of the rhetoric of business onto the world of crime in *American Buffalo* (1975); and it facilitates the appropriation of unquestioned values to the salesmen's patter in *Glengarry Glen Ross* (1983). Increasingly the dramatic context frames and ironizes linguistic opacity; the theatrical premise remains rooted in the radical loss of faith in language that occurred in the sixties.

The context of political radicalism implicit in that remark is pertinent to other eminent contemporary playwrights. August Wilson, for example, who achieved recognition with *Ma Rainey's Black Bottom* (1985) and has since won Pulitzer Prizes for *Fences* and *The Piano Lesson* (in 1987 and 1990), is a more introspective heir to the angry separatism of the Black Arts Movement. As well as the inevitable, acknowledged influence of Baraka, there are echoes of Bullins' twentieth-century cycle in his basically naturalistic dramas, which are nonetheless similarly conceived of as an allegorical history of the black experience through each decade of the twentieth century. Wilson's stature as a playwright rests squarely upon his own talents; but the process of racial self-examination his plays engage in is both more measured and more secure in addressing an establishment audience than would have been possible without the accumulated weight of oppositional radical black theatre. A similar argument might be advanced concerning contemporary women playwrights such as Wendy Wasserstein and Marsha Norman: both invoke the material of feminist polemics in their plays without finding it necessary to maintain a stance hostile to the theatrical establishment. Wasserstein, in *Uncommon Women and Others* (1978) and *Isn't It Romantic* (1983), was able to accommodate feminist themes to commercial success by wrapping them in the conciliatory ambience of comedy. Her 1989 Pulitzer Prize winning *The Heidi Chronicles* makes the same use of collusive wit (rather than the oppositional satire characteristic of radical theatre) to create empathy with a protagonist who functions less as a vehicle of feminism than as an exploration of the individual woman's problematic relation to that context. Marsha Norman, in *Getting Out* (1979) and *'night Mother* (1983, Pulitzer Prize), transforms feminist concerns into dramas of the human condition. In this way the establishment's anti-separatist demand for universalism is satisfied without negating the specificity of the female perspective: despite its exclusive focus upon the drama of a mother-daughter relationship, *'night Mother* was not perceived as a feminist play. While radical feminists remain suspicious of the terms of this canonization (noting, for example, that it depends upon a substitution of the isolated self for the communal emphasis of radical theatre groups), it nonetheless testifies to the effectiveness of their efforts to affirm the autonomy and intrinsic value of woman.

The radical theatres of the sixties and seventies were a vital and significant force for the interrogation of received notions of both the forms and the uses of theatre. Their persistent exploration of the latent possibilities in all aspects of the relation between theatre and life, individual and community, performance and experience, created an environment unusually rich in theatrical possibility. They produced some memorable theatre, and much more that is consigned to obscurity: but they also changed the ground on which theatre in general is created, and it is this enabling function of the radical theatre that is its most considerable legacy.

Guide to Further Reading

For full bibliographical details, see the appropriate references in the **Notes**, as indicated.

The most comprehensive guide to American radical theatre is volume three of C.W.E. Bigsby, *A Critical Introduction to Twentieth Century American*

Drama (Cambridge: Cambridge University Press, 1985), entitled *Beyond Broadway*, which includes extensive discussion of performance theatre and useful chapters on most of the other theatres treated here. Margaret Croyden, *Lunatics, Lovers and Poets*,[6] offers a more intimate perspective upon some of the same material, and is particularly good on performance theatre and its sources. James Roose-Evans, *Experimental Theatre from Stanislavsky to Today*, rev. ed. (London: Studio Vista, 1973), also offers chapters on the influence of Artaud and Grotowski, gives special notice to the Bread and Puppet Theatre, and surveys "America Today". A more detailed analysis of the range of American radical theatre is Theodore Shank, *American Alternative Theatre* (London: Macmillan, 1982). John Lahr, *Up Against the Fourth Wall*[8] is a valuable source for first hand accounts of performance theatre productions. Zoltan Szilassy, *American Theatre of the 1960s* (Carbondale: Southern Illinois University Press, 1986), provides an overview in the context of the Happenings and new performance theories, and takes notice of "regional alternative theatre". For discussions centred upon the playwright, see Ruby Cohn, *New American Dramatists 1960–1980* (London: Macmillan, 1982), who includes the Becks under this heading. A valuable reference work with a similar emphasis upon the playwright is D.L. Kirkpatrick, ed., *Contemporary Dramatists*.[29] Due to the nature of some of the theatre discussed eye-witness accounts of performances are a vital resource: Croyden, Shank and Lahr are valuable in this respect, as is Leslie Epstein, "Walking Wounded, Living Dead", *New American Review*, 6 (1969), 230–51, which is a detailed account of the Living Theatre's *Mysteries, Paradise Now, Antigone,* and *Frankenstein*. A useful anthology is John Lahr and Jonathan Price, eds., *The Great American Life Show*,[7] which includes *The Serpent* and the schedule of *Mysteries* as well as more readily available plays by Bullins and Baraka. *TDR* (*Tulane Drama Review/ The Drama Review*) is the most important periodical for both contemporary reviews of avant-garde performances and retrospective analysis. *Performing Arts Journal* has a great deal of valuable material, and *Theatre Quarterly* is occasionally useful. *The New York Times* also gave significant notice to many of the groups represented here.

The three essential sources for the Happenings are Michael Kirby, ed., *Happenings: An Illustrated Anthology*,[2] Allan Kaprow, *Assemblages, Environments & Happenings*,[3] and Richard Kostelanetz, *The Theatre of Mixed Means: An Introduction to Happenings, Kinetic Environments and Other Mixed-Means Performances* (1968; London: Pitman, 1970). Kirby includes an important introduction, statements by artists and descriptions of Happenings (including "18 Happenings in 6 Parts"); Kaprow's format is similar, but with little overlap of selected material. Both are generously illustrated. Kostelanetz provides a theoretical introduction that follows Kirby and Kaprow, and includes conversations with such figures as Cage, Halprin, Rauschenberg and Kaprow himself. Further contextualization is offered in Zoltan Szilassy, "The European Origins of Happenings and New Performance Theories", in Tibor Frank, ed., *The Origins and Originality of American Culture* (Budapest: Akademiai Kiado, 1984), pp. 431–8.

Two primary texts for the Living Theatre are Judith Malina, *The Enormous Despair* (New York: Random House, 1972), and Julian Beck, *The Life of the Theatre: the Relation of the Artist to the Struggle of the People* (San Francisco: City Lights, 1972). *TDR* published their interview with Richard Schechner, "Containment is the Enemy",[10] and *"Paradise Now Notes"*, *TDR*, 43 (1969), pp. 90–107. Another interview was published as "Radicalizing the Classics", *Performing Arts Journal*, 14 (1981), pp. 26–40. Periodical criticism includes Saul Gottlieb, "The Living Theatre in Exile", *TDR*, 32 (1966), pp. 137–52; Lyon Phelps, "Brecht at the Living Theatre", *TDR*, 37 (1967), pp. 125–31; an important review by Stefan Brecht, "Revolution at the Brooklyn Academy of Music", *TDR*, 43 (1969), pp. 46–73; and Paul Ryder Ryan, "The Living Theatre in Brazil", *TDR*, 51 (1971), pp. 21–30. Note also Leslie Epstein, as noted above, who is a valuable witness. Joseph Chaikin, *The Presence of the Actor*,[5] provides insights into the workings of the Open Theatre. Several Chaikin interviews are also worth consultation: "The Actor's Involvement", TDR, 38 (1968), pp. 147–51; interview and "Fragments", *TDR*, 43 (1969), pp. 141–7; and "Closing the Open Theatre", *Theatre Quarterly*, 16 (1974–5), pp. 36–43. Also relevant are Jean-Claude van Itallie, "Playwright at Work: Off Off-Broadway", *TDR*, 32 (1966), pp. 154–8; and Roberta Sklar, *"Terminal"*, interview, 149–157. Light on the Performance Group is provided by Richard Schechner's substantial theoretical writings, collected in *Public Domain*,[4] and *Performance Theory*, rev. and expanded ed. (New York: Routledge, 1988). Of particular importance are "6 Axioms for Environmental Theatre";[14] "Speculations on Sexuality, Performance and Politics", *TDR*, 44 (1969), pp. 89–110; "Audience Participation", *TDR*, 51 (1971), pp. 73–89; and the two-part "The Decline and Fall of the (American) Avant-Garde", *Performing Arts Journal*, 14 (1981), pp. 48–63, and 15 (1981), pp. 9–19. Stefan Brecht's running commentary on *Dionysus in 69*[11] is an essential critical review.

A good account of the black theatre of the period is provided by Geneviève Fabre, *Drumbeats, Masks, and Metaphor: Contemporary Afro-American Theatre*, trans. Melvin Dixon (Cambridge: Harvard University Press, 1983). Addison Gayle, Jr., ed., *The Black Aesthetic* (Garden City: Doubleday, 1971), has a useful drama section (pp. 263–330); and Harold Cruse, *The Crisis of the Negro Intellectual* (London: W.H. Allen, 1969) includes several chapters directly pertinent to the theatre. The development of feminist theatre is charted in Dinah Luise Leavitt, *Feminist Theatre Groups* (Jefferson: McFarland, 1980), and Elizabeth J.

Natalle, *Feminist Theatre: A Study in Persuasion* (Metuchen: Scarecrow Press, 1985); Jill Dolan, *The Feminist Spectator as Critic* (Ann Arbor: UMI Research Press, 1988), offers a more sophisticated theoretical analysis. The Theatre of the Ridiculous is most comprehensively treated in Stefan Brecht, *Queer Theatre* (1978; London: Methuen 1986), one of his series on "The Original Theatre of the City of New York: From the Mid-60s to the Mid-70s"; and a valuable interview with Charles Ludlam appeared in *Performing Arts Journal*.[20] Renate von Bardeleben, Dietrich Briesemeister and Juan Bruce-Novoa, eds., *Missions in Conflict: Essays on U.S.-Mexican Relations and Chicano Culture* (Tübingen: Narr, 1986), includes three essays on El Teatro Campesino, and Luis Valdez' own perspective in the early years is represented in "Teatro Campesino: Interview", *TDR*, 36 (1967), pp. 70–80. An essential source for the San Francisco Mime Troupe is by founder R.G. Davis, *The San Francisco Mime Troupe: The First Ten Years* (Palo Alto: Ramparts Press, 1975); see also his exercise in self definition against performance theatre, "The Radical Right in the American Theatre".[1] The causes of his split with the group are set out in "Politics, Art, and the San Francisco Mime Troupe", *Theatre Quarterly*, 18 (1975), pp. 26–7; and responded to by Joan Holden, "Collective Playmaking: the Why and the How".[21] Holden's case is supported by Theodore Shank, "Political Theatre: The San Francisco Mime Troupe", *TDR*, 61 (1974), pp. 110–17. The Bread and Puppet Theatre is exhaustively treated in Stefan Brecht, *Peter Schumann's Bread and Puppet Theatre* (London: Methuen, 1988), two fat volumes of Brecht's dense annotational prose. Peter Schumann's important interview, "The Bread and Puppet Theatre",[22] can be supplemented by his "Bread and Puppets", *TDR*, 47 (1970), p. 35; the same issue includes George Dennison's review of *Fire*, pp. 36–43, and a substantial essay by Stefan Brecht, "Peter Schumann's Bread and Puppet Theatre", pp. 44–90. See also John Townsen's review, "Bread and Puppet's *Stations of the Cross*", *TDR*, 55 (1972), pp. 57–70; and especially Florence Falk, "Bread and Puppet: Domestic Resurrection Circus".[24]

Robert Wilson's work is well analyzed from close range in Stefan Brecht, *The Theatre of Visions: Robert Wilson*.[25] See also Louis Aragon, "An Open Letter to André Breton … on Robert Wilson's *Deafman Glance*", *Performing Arts Journal*, 1 (1976), pp. 3–7. Richard Foreman's own essays are essential to an understanding of his theatre: see *Reverberation Machines*,[30] which includes playscripts. Kate Davy, *Richard Foreman and the Ontological-Hysteric Theatre* (Ann Arbor: UMI Research Press, 1981), is the best critical analysis, including useful illustrations and descriptions of performances. See also Michael Kirby, "Richard Foreman's Ontological-Hysteric Theatre", *TDR*, 58 (1973), pp. 5–32; and Florence Falk, "Ontological-Hysteric Theater: Setting as Consciousness", *Performing Arts Journal*, 1 (1976), pp. 51–61.

Notes

1. R. G. Davis, "The Radical Right in the American Theatre", *Theatre Quarterly*, 19 (1975), p. 67.
2. Michael Kirby, ed., *Happenings: An Illustrated Anthology* (London: Sidgwick and Jackson, 1965).
3. Allan Kaprow, *Assemblages, Environments & Happenings* (New York: Abrams, n. d. [1966]), p. 195.
4. Richard Schechner, "Exit Thirties, Enter Sixties", in *Public Domain: Essays on the Theatre* (Indianapolis: Bobbs-Merrill, 1969), p. 7.
5. Joseph Chaikin, *The Presence of the Actor* (New York: Atheneum, 1969).
6. Jerzy Grotowski, 1969 interview quoted in Margaret Croyden, *Lunatics, Lovers and Poets: The Contemporary Experimental Theatre* (New York: McGraw-Hill, 1974), p. 166.
7. Jean-Claude van Itallie, *The Serpent*, in John Lahr and Jonathan Price, eds., *The Great American Life Show: 9 Plays From the Avant-Garde Theatre* (New York: Bantam, 1974), p. 94.
8. Joseph Chaikin, quoted in John Lahr, *Up Against the Fourth Wall: Essays on Modern Theater* (New York: Grove, 1970), p. 173.
9. Antonin Artaud, *The Theater and Its Double*, trans. Mary Caroline Richards (New York: Grove Press, 1958), p. 124.
10. Judith Malina and Julian Beck, "Containment is the Enemy", interview with Richard Schechner, *TDR*, 43 (1969), pp. 24–5.
11. Stefan Brecht, rev. of *Dionysus in 69*, TDR, 43 (1969), p. 163.
12. "Containment is the Enemy", p. 35.
13. *Ibid.*, p. 34.
14. Richard Schechner, "6 Axioms for Environmental Theatre", 39 (1968), p. 50.
15. "Containment is the Enemy", p. 26.
16. Rev. of *Paradise Now*, *New York Times*, 28 Sept. 1969, p. 27.
17. *The Theater and Its Double*, p. 126.
18. *Ibid.*, p. 7.
19. *The Presence of the Actor*, p. 25.
20. Charles Ludlam, interview, *Performing Arts Journal*, 3 (Spring/Summer 1978), p. 78.
21. Joan Holden, "Collective Playmaking: the Why and the How", *Theatre Quarterly*, 18 (1975), p. 30.
22. Peter Schumann, "With the Bread and Puppet Theatre", interview, TDR, 38 (1968), p. 64.
23. *Ibid.*, p. 70.
24. Schumann, quoted in Florence Falk, "Bread and Puppet: Domestic Resurrection Circus", *Performing Arts Journal*, 2 (Spring

1977), pp. 20–21.

25. Stefan Brecht, *The Theatre of Visions: Robert Wilson* (1978; Frankfurt: Suhrkamp, 1989), p. 9.

26. *Ibid.*, p. 10.

27. Richard Foreman, rev. of *The Life and Times of Sigmund Freud*, *Village Voice*, 1 Jan. 1970, rpt. in *The Theatre of Visions*, p. 425.

28. *Ibid.*, p. 427.

29. Richard Foreman, quoted in D. L. Kirkpatrick, ed., *Contemporary Dramatists*, 4th ed. (Chicago: St. James Press, 1988), p. 157.

30. Richard Foreman, *Reverberation Machines: Later Plays and Essays* (New York: Station Hill, 1985), p. viii.

31. *Ibid*, p. 239.

32. *Contemporary Dramatists*, p. 157.

33. *Reverberation Machines*, pp. 190–1

34. *Ibid.*, p. 235.

35. *Ibid.*, p. 191.

36. *Ibid.*, p. 190.

37. *Ibid.*, p. 238.

38. *Ibid.*, p. 193.

39. Richard Schechner, "The Decline and Fall of the (American) Avant-Garde, *Performing Arts Journal*, 15 (1981), pp. 11–12.

BAAS PAMPHLETS IN AMERICAN STUDIES

BAAS PAMPHLETS IN AMERICAN STUDIES

ORDER BAAS PAMPHLETS FROM RYBURN DISTRIBUTION,
Tenterfields, Luddendenfoot, Halifax HX2 6EJ, England
For ordering details please see overleaf

RYBURN BAAS AMERICAN LIBRARY

The classic of plantation slavery rediscovered —

DRED:
A TALE OF THE GREAT DISMAL SWAMP
by Harriet Beecher Stowe
Edited by Judie Newman

752 pages, 174 x 115mm
Paperback ISBN 1 85331 038 7
Bonded Leather ISBN 1 85331 025 5

The Ryburn BAAS American Library is a reprint series of significant but difficult-to-obtain texts freshly edited by experts specially selected by Ryburn Publishing in association with the British Association for American Studies

ORDER BAAS PAMPHLETS AND RYBURN-BAAS BOOKS
FROM YOUR BOOKSELLER OR DIRECT FROM

RYBURN DISTRIBUTION,
Tenterfields, Luddendenfoot, Halifax HX2 6EJ, England
Payment by Access/MasterCard and Visa is accepted: please quote credit card number, expiry date and address at which registered. Credit cards will be debited in £ sterling prices on dispatch of order. If not paying by credit card, non-account customers must enclose payment with order. Postage and packing is charged extra at 10% retail value of order with a minimum charge of £1 and a maximum of £10. Pamphlet orders may be combined with orders for Ryburn books.